The KidHaven Science Library

Monsoons

by Peggy J. Parks

KIDHAVEN PRESS

An imprint of Thomson Gale, a part of The Thomson Corporation

THOMSON
™
GALE

Detroit • New York • San Francisco • New Haven, Conn. • Waterville, Maine • London

For more information, contact
KidHaven Press
27500 Drake Rd.
Farmington Hills, MI 48331-3535
Or you can visit our Internet site at http://www.gale.com

LIBRARY OF CONGRESS CATALOGING-IN-PUBLICATION DATA

Parks, Peggy J., 1951–
Monsoons / by Peggy J. Parks.
    p. cm. — (KidHaven science library) Includes bibliographical references and index.
ISBN-13: 978-0-7377-3058-6 (hardcover : alk. paper)
ISBN-10: 0-7377-3058-7 (hardcover : alk. paper)
1. Monsoons—Juvenile literature.   I. Title.
QC939.M7P123 2006
551.51'84—dc22   2006020801

Contents

Chapter 1

"The Air Is on Fire"

Each year in late May, the people of southern Asia await the **monsoon** with great excitement. After months of blazing heat, they hope and pray that the monsoon will bring much-needed rain. One country where this is especially true is India, which is one of the hottest places on Earth. Writer Karada Shantipriya explains what it is like in India just before the monsoon arrives: The ground is dry and parched under the scorching rays of the sun. The air is on fire and the leaves are perfectly still as if holding their breath. . . . In a sudden moment, the sky darkens and the sun is lost behind a blanket of grey clouds. The leaves flutter excitedly in the cool breeze. The clouds melt as the earth thirstily drinks in the first drops of rain. The monsoon has arrived.[1]

Fierce Rainstorms

Monsoon rains in Asia are very different from rainfall in most other parts of the world. Monsoon rain often comes in the form of **torrential** downpours. For instance, on July 26, 2005, as much as 37 inches (94cm) of rain fell in the Indian city of Mumbai (formerly known as Bombay) in just 24 hours. That is about the same amount of rain that falls on American cities such as Washington, D.C., or Seattle in an entire year.

Another characteristic of monsoon rain is that it can drag on for weeks at a time. Venu Madhav Govindu,

Scorched earth in northern India soaks up welcome moisture when the monsoon season arrives.

People wade through flooded streets in Mumbai, India, during monsoon rains in July 2005.

a writer from Goa, India, experienced this during the summer of 2003. In an article entitled "My Monsoons," he describes the "endless sheets of rain"[2] that began in early June and lasted for an entire month. "It is mid-July and the heavens have literally opened up here,"[3] writes Govindu. During the summer, some parts of India receive as much as 40 feet (12m) of rain as a direct result of the monsoon.

These heavy monsoon rainstorms often lead to severe flooding, which was the case in Mumbai during late July 2005. The rain fell so fast that the streets flooded quickly, crippling the busy city's traffic flow. Anjali Krishnan was driving to a meeting during the fierce rainstorm. The water in the streets was rising rapidly, and soon her car became stranded.

After staying in her car for ten hours, Krishnan decided to try walking home. Many other people had made the same decision, and they held hands to keep from slipping beneath the deep water. This was difficult as well as dangerous, as Krishnan explains: "The water was black and greasy right up to our necks and swirled fast around our waists. . . . I had forgotten the tiredness, the grime, the potential dangers that such flooding held."[4] Krishnan spent more than three hours wading through the neck-deep water before she finally made it home safely.

Ancient Wisdom

Because such heavy rainfall is closely connected with monsoons, people often think the word monsoon means "rain," but it does not. Monsoons are actually seasonal wind shifts, rather than precipitation. The word comes from the Arabic word *mausim*, which means "season of winds."

Ancient traders sailing through the Indian Ocean and adjoining Arabian Sea used *mausim* to refer to the wind patterns they encountered during their travels. They observed that the winds varied depending on the season of the year. During the winter months, for instance, it blew mainly from the northeast. In the summer it shifted direction and blew from the southwest. The voyagers used this knowledge to plan their journeys through the ocean. By doing so, they could use the powerful winds to propel their sailboats.

Forces of Nature

Today, scientists know much more about monsoons than the voyagers of long ago did. But they also know the ancient travelers were correct—monsoon winds do change direction based on the season. Thus, scientists refer to two different types of monsoons: summer and winter.

During the summer monsoon, warm, wet winds blow from the ocean toward the land. In the winter, winds shift and travel from the land toward the ocean. The winter monsoon in Asia lasts from December to early March. During those months, there is little or no rainfall. As the wind blows over the land and heads toward the water, it picks up soil, sand, and dust. This often leads to severe dust storms.

In China, Asia's largest country, dust storms are common during the winter monsoon. Raging winds pick up millions of tons of sand and dust from the northern China desert. The yellowish dust fills the air for weeks at a time. It sifts through windows and

During a winter dust storm in Beijing, China, monsoon winds whip the flags in Tiananmen Square.

doors and coats everything in its path, from cars and buses to buildings, sidewalks, and roads.

In March 2006, the worst dust storm in five years struck China's capital city of Beijing. About 300,000 tons (272,000 metric tons) of dust was dumped on the city. It was so thick that people could not see, and it completely blocked out the sky for days. Then the thick plume of dust drifted along in the wind, traveling east toward Japan and Korea. When it reached South Korea, it mingled with **precipitation** in the clouds to produce ugly brownish-yellow snow.

Beyond Asia

Although the biggest and best-known monsoons occur in various parts of the Asian continent, smaller monsoons occur in other parts of the world as well. Central Africa experiences monsoons, as does northern Australia. There are even monsoons in the southwestern United States. Arizona, for instance, has one monsoon each year that lasts from July through mid-September. During these hot, dry summer months, shifting winds pull up moisture from the Gulf of California and the Gulf of Mexico. This produces severe changes in weather.

As they do in China, monsoon winds can stir up raging dust storms in Arizona. Sometimes these storms whip up towering walls of dust known as **haboobs**. They can grow to be enormous—several miles long and thousands of feet high. Nancy Ahern, an Arizona resident who lives near Tucson, once

Violent thunderstorms (right) often follow the dust storms of Arizona's monsoons, leading to flash floods (top).

faced such a dust storm. She describes the experience: "You see it coming. You see the monster piles of black clouds gathering about the edges of the horizon and then the air gets a leaden tinge to it. While the breeze picks up, you see the wall of brown chugging toward you. It's unbelievable—and scary."[5]

The dust storms of Arizona's monsoon are often followed by violent thunderstorms. Heavy rains can lead to sudden, unpredictable floods known as **flash floods**. They are especially dangerous in deep, narrow canyons. When water starts washing into these areas, it rises extremely fast because there is no way for it to drain quickly. This happened in Arizona's Antelope Canyon during August 1997. Eleven people hiking there were caught in a flash flood. Without warning, they were overcome by a gigantic wall of water that rushed toward them with incredible force. All of the hikers were swept away to their deaths. Rescue workers later recovered a camera that had belonged to one of them. A photo showed that the water had been more than 50 feet (15m) high.

"Perfect Harmony"

Monsoons have a major effect on climate and precipitation. They can be unpredictable as well as frightening, and sometimes they are dangerous. But to people like Shantipriya, the monsoon is nothing short of magical. He writes: "The wind and the rain, the thunder and lightning, all play in perfect harmony, striking up a symphony in nature."[6]

Chapter 2

The Making of a Monsoon

Monsoons occur only in some areas of the world because they need certain features in order to form. One of those features is a large area of land known as a landmass. The places that experience monsoons have very hot, tropical climates. The blazing sun beats down day after day, warming the land with its intense heat. The larger the landmass, the greater the amount of heat that it can absorb from the Sun.

In addition to a landmass, the other feature that is necessary for a monsoon to form is an ocean. Earth's oceans cover nearly 75 percent of the planet's surface. Like land, they also absorb the heat from the Sun. But oceans are such vast bodies of water that they absorb the heat more slowly. It takes much longer for them to warm up than it does land.

A Monsoon Is Born

Because the land and oceans warm up at different rates of speed, this can result in sharp temperature

Formation of Summer Monsoons

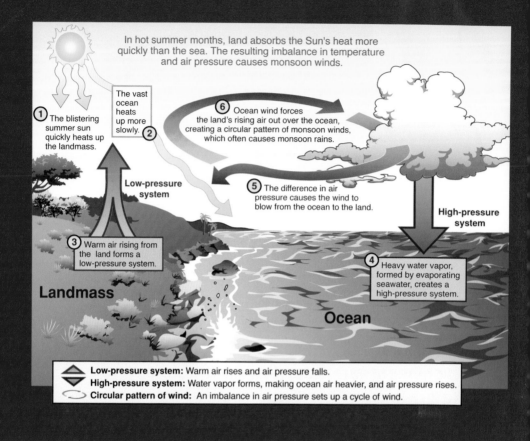

In hot summer months, land absorbs the Sun's heat more quickly than the sea. The resulting imbalance in temperature and air pressure causes monsoon winds.

1 The blistering summer sun quickly heats up the landmass.

The vast ocean heats up more slowly. **2**

6 Ocean wind forces the land's rising air out over the ocean, creating a circular pattern of monsoon winds, which often causes monsoon rains.

Low-pressure system

5 The difference in air pressure causes the wind to blow from the ocean to the land.

High-pressure system

3 Warm air rising from the land forms a low-pressure system.

4 Heavy water vapor, formed by evaporating seawater, creates a high-pressure system.

Landmass

Ocean

Low-pressure system: Warm air rises and air pressure falls.
High-pressure system: Water vapor forms, making ocean air heavier, and air pressure rises.
Circular pattern of wind: An imbalance in air pressure sets up a cycle of wind.

differences between them. During the summer months, when the Sun is at its hottest, the land absorbs heat quickly. As a result, the land becomes warmer than the sea. The land temperature continues to increase, which causes stored heat reflecting off the surface to warm the air above it. This causes the air to expand, moving its **molecules** farther apart and making the air lighter. The heated air begins to rise, causing the air pressure to fall. This creates what is known as a **low-pressure system** near the land's surface.

Meanwhile, the opposite is happening over the ocean, and a **high-pressure system** is developing. As the Sun's heat warms the water, huge amounts of seawater evaporate into the air. During this process, the water changes into a gas known as **water vapor**. Because of all the moisture, the air above the ocean becomes much more humid than air over the land. Air molecules move closer together, making the oceanic air heavier. The air pressure rises, and this results in the ocean's high-pressure system.

This difference in temperature and air pressure between water and land creates an imbalance of energy. Whenever there is any sort of imbalance, it is quickly corrected by nature. Air naturally begins to blow from the high-pressure area (the ocean) to the low-pressure area (the land). This movement of air is known as wind.

As winds blow away from the ocean, a thick layer of damp ocean air settles over the land. This causes the warm air above the land to be pushed upward. At the same time, the rising air from the landmass is drawn outward over the ocean to replace the oceanic air that has moved inland. This creates a circular process that continues on and on, fueled by the energy of the Sun. The result is a constant flow of moist ocean air toward the land.

Monsoon Rain

An important part of the cycle is how precipitation is created. When cooler oceanic air forces the land's

A colorful train passes through farmlands flooded during India's record-breaking 2005 monsoon season.

warm air upward, the air rises into the atmosphere and it, too, cools. This cooling process causes the water vapor in the air to **condense**, or change back to a liquid form. Condensation creates tiny droplets of water that cluster together. When billions of these droplets are combined, they form clouds.

The air inside the clouds continues to cool, which makes more water vapor condense to create even more water droplets. Eventually, the clouds become so heavy that they cannot hold the moisture—and that is when the monsoon rains begin to fall. In some areas of the world, the ongoing circulation of air between the ocean and land creates nearly constant rainfall. Because of the drenching rains that typically accompany summer monsoons, they are often called wet monsoons.

"Unmistakably Indian"

Nowhere on Earth are conditions more ideal for such monsoons than India—and they are more dramatic and intense than monsoons found anywhere else in the world. Shantipriya writes: "With its life-giving rain and its wild storms, the monsoon is . . . whimsical, unpredictable and unmistakably Indian."[7] Even though the people of India expect the monsoon every year, it can still surprise them when it occurs. The weather may be unbearably hot and dry one minute, and then suddenly the skies open up and rain pours down on the parched land.

A major factor in the formation of India's monsoons is its enormous area of land. It is a huge country, covering more than 1 million square miles

During India's 2005 monsoon, a man braves chest-high flood waters to rescue four puppies.

The massive Himalaya mountain range on India's northern border strongly influences the country's climate.

(2.6 million sq km). India is also a peninsula, meaning it is surrounded on three sides by large bodies of water: the Indian Ocean to the south, the Arabian Sea to the west, and the Bay of Bengal to the east. The temperature difference between India's landmass and these bodies of water can be dramatic. It is not uncommon for land temperatures to exceed 113°F (45°C), while the water temperature in the adjacent oceans averages about 68°F (20°C).

India's climate is another essential factor in monsoon development. The climate is greatly influenced by the Himalaya mountain range, which borders India on the north. The Himalayas are the tallest mountains on Earth. They stretch for 1,700 miles (2,700km), with towering peaks nearly 26,000 feet (8,000m) high. The mountain range is one major reason why India's climate is so hot. It forms a barrier that prevents the cold north winds of central Asia from reaching the Indian **subcontinent**. Also, India's location is a factor in its scorching climate. Much of the country lies between the **Tropic of Cancer** and the equator, so the Sun shines directly on the land for much of the year.

Climate Shift

During September, the climate starts to grow cooler in India and other southwestern Asian countries. This temperature change marks the end of the summer monsoon and the start of the winter monsoon. Although these regions are still very hot for

The Monsoons of India

Several factors in India provide ideal conditions for the formation of monsoons. India's monsoons are the most powerful of any on Earth.

The blazing Sun heats the land and—to a lesser extent—the surrounding bodies of water.

TIBET

The world's highest mountain chain, the Himalayas, protects India from the cold winds of central Asia.

PAKISTAN

NEPAL

BHUTAN

Himalayas

BANGLADESH

Tropic of Cancer

I N D I A

MYANMAR

India is a huge country, more than one-third the size of the United States.

Bay of Bengal

Arabian Sea

Because much of India lies in the tropical climate zone between the equator and the Tropic of Cancer, the Sun shines directly on the land for much of the year.

Indian Ocean

SRI LANKA

India is a peninsula, surrounded by large bodies of water on three sides.

Equator

The features that must be present for ideal monsoon conditions are: a large landmass, an ocean, and a hot climate. India has them all.

most of the year, the Sun's heat is less intense during the fall and winter.

As temperatures drop, the land cools down as well. The ocean, however, does not cool as quickly as the land. Because of its vast size, it is able to store the Sun's heat for long periods of time. Thus, during the winter months, the ocean remains warmer than the land.

Just as imbalances are corrected by nature during the summer, the same is true during the winter months—only in reverse. A layer of air over the ocean becomes warmer than the air over the land. A high-pressure system develops over the land, and a low-pressure system develops over the ocean. Winds form and blow the air away from the land toward the sea.

Winter monsoons typically have little or no precipitation, which is why they are often called dry monsoons. Also, the temperature difference between the ocean and land is less extreme than in the summer. As a result, winds during the winter monsoon are not as strong, nor as constant.

Monsoons form because of a unique interaction between land and sea. Although the summer and winter monsoons are often different from each other, they are both examples of the immense power of nature.

Chapter 3

A Matter of Life and Death

In regions of the world where monsoons occur, they are a mixed blessing. Their torrential rains can be destructive and deadly, causing severe flooding and landslides. But monsoon rains also provide relief from months of blazing hot temperatures. They quench the thirst of dry, parched land and replenish water supplies that help sustain people throughout the dry season. For those whose lives depend on the monsoon, the arrival of the rain is an event to celebrate. As Govindu explains: "Breaking out after a long, harsh summer the monsoon is life giving. On its timeliness and generosity hinges the hopes and lives of millions of people."[8]

A Precious Resource

Most of the people who are dependent on the monsoon live in Asian countries. In India alone, where the population is more than a billion, almost 90 percent of the water supply comes from monsoon rains. Because the monsoon lasts only for several months, people must do whatever they can to save the rainwater. In Laporiya, for instance, a village in the Indian state of Rajasthan, residents practice what is known as **rainwater harvesting**. They use large irrigation tanks and other modern storage methods to save the water so it can be used during dry periods.

The people of Pakistan, another Asian country, also rely on monsoon rains for much of their water. In one area, the Thar Desert, monsoon rainfall is the only source of freshwater. Pakistan's climate is

A system of irrigation canals in the Indian state of Rajasthan is one of the largest such projects in the world.

drier than India's, and its rainfall is even scarcer. When the monsoon finally arrives, people in the Thar region do everything possible to catch and store the rainwater. They use earthen jars as well as underground tanks. Farmers dig ditches or pits to hold rainwater so they can irrigate crops after the monsoon has ended.

"Water Gives Us Life"

People who live in Cambodia, an Asian country located between Thailand and Vietnam, benefit from an unusual occurrence during the summer monsoon. The heavy rains cause a complete rever-

A festive boat participates in the Cambodian water festival, which celebrates the reversal of the Tonle Sap River.

sal of a Cambodian river's current. From November through May, the Tonle Sap River feeds into the Mekong River. But when summer monsoon rains swell the Mekong, the excess water spills into the Tonle Sap. For some mysterious reason, this abundance of water causes the river to start flowing backward.

Water from the river starts pouring into Tonle Sap Lake in western Cambodia. The Tonle Sap is the largest freshwater lake in Southeast Asia. During the summer monsoon, the lake swells to more than five times its normal size. The swollen lake provides the ideal breeding ground for many different types of fish. As a result of the monsoon rains, Tonle Sap Lake becomes one of the most productive fisheries in the world.

For Cambodians, this is a great blessing because fish makes up about 70 percent of their diet. They celebrate the monsoon by holding a three-day water festival known as Bonn Om Touk. Each year, more than a million people from all over Cambodia flock to the annual event. Journalist Kay Kimsong expresses how grateful the Cambodian people are for the monsoon rains: "Thanks to the water. . . . The water provides many things—water gives us life."[9]

Creatures of the Monsoon

Just as monsoon rains are vital for humans, they also ensure the survival of wildlife. Animals in many parts of the world are able to sense when

The eggs of gharial crocodiles are laid and hatch during the monsoon rainy season.

the monsoon is due to arrive. Often, their living, mating, and eating habits revolve around the monsoon. A PBS article entitled "Monsoon" describes two of these creatures: "Indian elephants feast upon the fresh grass shoots nourished by the monsoon, while a host of birds flock to the lengthening stems to build their nest."[10]

One bird that benefits from the monsoon is known as the lesser florican. It resembles a chicken and is one of the rarest birds in the world. The male florican thrives in the rain-soaked meadow grasses. It must find a mate before the monsoon rain ends and the grasses become parched and dry—which is no easy challenge. The bird is only about 1.5 feet (.5m) tall, much too short to be visible in the tall meadow grass. So about every three minutes, it leaps above the tall grass in the hope of impressing a mate. In one day, the male florican may jump as many as 600 times!

Another creature that thrives because of the Asian monsoon is the gharial crocodile. These huge creatures, which live in northern Indian rivers, can grow to be about 23 feet (7m) long. When monsoon rains arrive, the rivers flood and the banks become saturated with water. The wet, sandy riverbanks provide an ideal place for the crocodiles to lay their eggs. When the eggs hatch, the baby gharials climb out to find their mothers, who are waiting nearby to protect them.

The Deadly Side of Monsoons

As helpful as monsoon rains can be, however, they do not only give life—they can also take it away. One of the greatest risks of these rains is flooding. Each year, floods throughout Asia cause widespread damage to farms by washing away crops and drowning livestock. They also cause landslides that can sweep away entire villages.

Such a tragedy occurred in July 2005. Heavy rains drenched the Indian state of Maharashtra, killing more than a thousand people. Most of them drowned or were killed in landslides. Tens of thousands were left homeless.

One of the victims was Muhammed Rizwan, who lived in a rural village not far from Mumbai. He fought his way through the flooded streets, only to find that his home had been buried by a huge landslide from a nearby hill. Forty people had been killed in the landslide, including Rizwan's wife and three children.

Shanta Bai, a woman who lived in the village of Gautam Nagar, was another victim of the summer 2005 flood. She describes how devastating the tragedy was for her: "My house was flooded with water. I survived without food for two days. I have lost everything. What will I do?"[11]

Floods and Drought

Some of the most deadly monsoon floods have occurred in China, along the Yangtze River. In fact, the worst natural disaster in Chinese history struck the country during the summer of 1931. Monsoon rains swelled the Yangtze, along with two other great rivers, the Yellow and the Huaihe. The powerful force of the water caused more than a thousand **levees**, or protective barriers, to burst. Water began gushing over the riverbanks, flooding nearly 62,000 square miles (160,000 sq km) of land. That is an area equal to the size of New York, New Jersey, and Connecticut combined. As many as 3.7 million people died as a result of the flood. Tens of thousands of the victims drowned in their own beds.

Although monsoon floods can bring death and destruction, an even greater danger is drought. When the monsoon brings no rain, farmers cannot plant crops and food supplies dwindle. This can lead to famine, or mass starvation. One of the worst famines of all time occurred in 1877. When

In India, a girl holds two kerosene lanterns aloft as she makes her way through flooded streets.

Forced to leave her flooded home in northern India, a woman carries her son to safety.

a monsoon bypassed parts of China, there was no rain for growing crops. Tragically, more than 10 million people starved to death.

Monsoons can bring death as well as life. Still, people hope and pray for the monsoon—and when it finally arrives, they celebrate. As unpredictable as it can be, without the monsoon they would have little chance of survival.

Chapter 4

What Can Be Done?

Because monsoons are a force of nature, no one can control or influence them. But through research, scientists hope to increase their knowledge and understanding of monsoons. **Climatologist** David Stephenson explains: "Because of the intensity of the weather, [monsoons] are a natural laboratory for scientists to observe the way the land, sea, and atmosphere . . . interact with each other and influence weather."[12] The studies will hopefully lead to more accurate forecasting, including the ability to predict where and when the rains will fall. This is a crucial step in helping people prepare for monsoons and better cope with their effects.

"Throwing of the Dice"

Such forecasting, however, is no easy task. Monsoon formation is completely dependent on natural forces whose behavior can change suddenly and abruptly. This can sometimes lead to highly inaccurate predictions.

An example of flawed forecasting took place in India during the summer 2005 monsoon. Scientists

A TV crew films gathering monsoon clouds over Mumbai, where Indian meteorologists failed to predict a massive monsoon downpour in 2005.

at the India Meteorological Department (IMD) used a **computer model** to estimate the timing and extent of the monsoon. Computer models are complex programs that **simulate** how atmospheric conditions will likely change over time. The IMD model analyzed sixteen different **meteorological** factors that could affect monsoon formation, from air temperatures to wind patterns.

When the analysis was complete, scientists predicted a normal monsoon for India—but their forecast was wrong. Over the course of the monsoon, India's rainfall was 30 percent lower than normal.

In addition, the model failed to predict a massive downpour in Mumbai, which was the worst storm in a hundred years.

IMD scientists were criticized for their inaccurate findings. Some of the critics insisted that the group's predictions failed because its technology was out of date. Dev Raj Sikka, one of the inventors of the computer model, does not agree. He maintains that monsoon prediction is a "gamble whose [accuracy is just barely] above the throwing of the dice."[13] Still, in light of the error, Sikka and other IMD scientists are working hard to improve their forecasting models.

Sikka's view about the challenge of forecasting is shared by Harold Brooks, a scientist with the U.S. National Severe Storms Laboratory. He says that forecasting is largely based on past events that have occurred frequently. According to Brooks, it is nearly impossible for scientists to predict highly unusual occurrences, such as a fierce rainstorm that occurs only once per century.

Forecasting for Farming

Although monsoon forecasting is not always accurate, many scientists believe it has great potential. One of them is Chris Thorncroft, a scientist from Albany, New York. Thorncroft works with an international organization that studies monsoons and their impact. The group uses satellite technology and other equipment to perfect forecasting techniques.

Thorncroft says that accurately predicting monsoons would be especially valuable for farmers. Armed with such information, they could alter their farming methods to help limit the impact of drought and flooding. "You can perhaps change the plant that you sow," says Thorncroft. "Or you can change the time that you seed crops depending on whether the rains will come late, or not come at all."[14]

Peter Webster, an American climate researcher, agrees that accurate forecasting of monsoons is crucial. He has developed a computer model that he believes could greatly improve such forecasting. Webster says the technology could also help increase crop yields in Asia and Africa. He used the system to generate 20- to 25-day rainfall forecasts for a region in Bangladesh, a country in southern Asia. The resulting forecasts were quite accurate, closely mirroring actual precipitation for the season. Webster says that in the future, such forecasts could guide farmers in choosing the best planting times. They could also help farmers make other decisions that affect crop production, such as how to better manage water.

A Warming Earth

Even with advanced technology, forecasting is tricky because monsoons are so unpredictable. From one year to the next, they do not necessarily behave the same way. Some scientists are convinced that monsoons are becoming more unpredictable because

This meteorological satellite will help scientists predict monsoons and other weather events.

The burning of this tropical forest to make way for new farmland creates carbon dioxide.

of **global warming**, which is a steady increase in the earth's temperature. Since 1900, the average global temperature has increased by about 1°F (.6°C). Although that does not sound like much of a change, a growing number of scientists are concerned about it. They fear that it is being caused by human actions, such as releasing too much **carbon dioxide** (CO_2) to the atmosphere.

CO_2 is created whenever large areas of tropical forest are cleared and burned. An even greater amount is produced by the burning of **fossil fuels** such as coal, oil, and natural gas. As the world's population continues to grow, more and more CO_2 is being pumped into the atmosphere. Scientists who are concerned about global warming believe there is a strong connection between the increased CO_2 and the warming of the planet. They warn that this change in worldwide climate could influence the behavior of natural events such as monsoons.

Scientist Jonathan Overpeck believes there is a link between the temperature of the North Atlantic Ocean and the Asian monsoon. His research shows that the ocean is becoming cooler, likely because glaciers and other large ice formations are rapidly melting into it. Overpeck says that such changes in seawater temperature could reduce the strength of future monsoons. He explains: "If the North Atlantic should cool without warning, one of the results could be a weakened monsoon and less water for all the people that depend on it. . . . Either way you look at it, global warming could . . . generate substantial human suffering."[15]

Conserving Precious Water

Scientists are not positive that global warming affects monsoons. But they do know that monsoons can be difficult to predict. Therefore, it is more important than ever that people learn how to cope with scarce rainfall. A major part of that is water **conservation**.

An India-based organization called the Centre for Science and Environment wants to create awareness of the importance of water harvesting. One of the group's major projects is the creation of "raincentres." These exhibitions teach the Indian people how to conserve and save water by harvesting rain. They show the importance of rain to the Indian way of life. They also show Indian citizens how they can all play an important role in rainwater conservation.

Chaukas

Many regions throughout India have developed their own rainwater harvesting programs. One of them is the town of Laporiya. During the 1970s, the pastures were barren and unable to support any crops. But that is not true today. The people of the village built a system of *chaukas*, or rectangular plots, that were designed to manage rainwater. The *chaukas* are about 200 feet (61m) long by 400 feet (122m) wide, and are arranged in a zigzag pattern. Whenever it rains, water collects in a *chauka*. As the amount of water stored in the enclosure rises, it spills into the next *chauka*. During the process of spilling from one *chauka* to another, the water gradually seeps onto the pasture. This ensures that crops are watered gradually and are not flooded with too much water at once. At the end of the line, the excess water runs into a special drain to be used for the village water supply.

Rainwater harvesting in the Indian town of Laporiya has resulted in the greening of formerly barren farmland.

Nature's Power

Monsoons are natural occurrences over which humans have no control. But as scientists continue to study monsoons, their knowledge and understanding continue to grow. With continued progress, the devastation that often accompanies monsoons could become a thing of the past.

Chapter 1: "The Air Is on Fire"

1. Karada Shantipriya, "Monsoon," Telugu Literary, October 13, 2005. www.teluguworld.org/Writers/Shantipriya/monsoon.html.
2. Venu Madhav Govindu, "Reflections: My Monsoons," Himal South Asian, August 2003. www.himālmag.com/2003/august/reflections_ 2.htm.
3. Govindu, "My Monsoons."
4. Anjali Krishnan, "Wading All Night Through Mumbai," BBC News, July 28, 2005. http://news.bbc.co.uk/2/hi/south_asia/4724245.stm.
5. Nancy Ahern, interview with the author, June 1, 2006.
6. Shantipriya, "Monsoon."

Chapter 2: The Making of a Monsoon

7. Shantipriya, "Monsoon."

Chapter 3: A Matter of Life and Death

8. Govindu, "My Monsoons."
9. Quoted in Michael Sullivan, "Tonle Sap: The Flowing Heart of Cambodia," NPR, December 6, 2005. www.npr.org/templates/story/story.php?storyId=5039980.

10. PBS, "Nature: Monsoon." www.pbs.org/wnet/ nature/monsoon/html/body_intro.html.
11. Quoted in Amit Kumar, "Rebuilding Lives Destroyed by the Indian Floods," International Federation of Red Cross, August 15, 2005. www.ifrc.org/docs/news/05/05081801.

Chapter 4: What Can Be Done?
12. Quoted in PBS, "Nature: Monsoon."
13. Quoted in Pallava Bagla, "Drought Exposes Cracks in India's Monsoon Model," *Science*, August 23, 2002, p. 1265 (2).
14. Quoted in Marc Airhart, "Interview: Scientist Looks to Africa for Hurricane Prediction," *Earth & Sky*, April 2005. www.earthsky.com/human world/interviews.php?id=44564.
15. Quoted in Shoshana Mayden, "Climate Records Show Global Warming Could Influence Asian Monsoon," *Science Daily*, January 27, 2003. www.sciencedaily.com/releases/2003/01/030 127075900.htm.

Glossary

carbon dioxide (CO_2): A gas that occurs naturally in the atmosphere and is also produced whenever forests and fossil fuels are burned.

climatologist: A scientist who studies climate.

computer model: A computer program that shows how atmospheric conditions will likely change over time.

condense: To change from a gas to a liquid as the result of being cooled.

conservation: Preserving and renewing natural resources such as water.

flash floods: Floods that occur rapidly, with no warning.

fossil fuels: Organic fuels (coal, oil, and natural gas) that were formed over millions of years from the remains of ancient plants and animals.

global warming: The steady increase of the planet's average temperature.

haboobs: Enormous walls of dust that are stirred up by extremely high winds.

high-pressure system: An area where the air molecules are packed closely together, making the air heavy and increasing atmospheric pressure.

levees: Protective barriers built along the banks of a river or lake to protect against flooding.

low-pressure system: An area where air molecules are scattered far apart, making the air light and decreasing atmospheric pressure.

meteorological: Having to do with meteorology, the study of the atmosphere or weather.

molecules: The smallest piece of a compound (such as water) that can exist. Molecules are made up of groups of atoms that form from the compounds.

monsoon: A seasonal wind shift that influences climate and precipitation.

precipitation: Any form of water—such as rain or snow—that falls to Earth.

rainwater harvesting: A method of capturing and storing rainwater.

simulate: To create a likeness of something.

subcontinent: A large landmass smaller than a continent.

torrential: Pouring freely or rapidly.

Tropic of Cancer: The northernmost point on Earth where the Sun is directly overhead.

water vapor: Water that exists in the form of a gas.

For Further Exploration

Books

Rachel Eagen, *Flood and Monsoon Alert!* New York: Crabtree, 2005. A book about monsoon rains—their ability to help sustain life and their destructive power.

Uma Krishnaswami, *Monsoon.* New York: Farrar, Strauss, and Giroux, 2003. A beautifully illustrated book that describes monsoon rains through the eyes of a child. Includes information about monsoons and how important the rains are to the people of India.

Periodicals

L. Balasubramaniam, "The Indian Monsoon," *Children's World*, July 1999, pp. 29–32.

Crinkles, "Monsoons: A Blustery Cycle," November/December 2000, pp. 29–32.

Internet Sources

Jill Egan, "Monsoons Soak Mumbai, India," *Time for Kids*, August 1, 2005. www.timeforkids.com/TFK/news/story/0,6260,1089019,00.html.

National Geographic Student Atlas, "Natural World: Monsoons." http://java.nationalgeographic.com/student atlas/clickup/monsoons.html.

Neepah Shah, "Floods Sweep Across South Asia," *Time for Kids*, July 16, 2004. www.timeforkids.com/TFK/news/story/0,6260,664067,00.html.

Web Sites

Mr. Dowling.com, Monsoon (www.mrdowling.com/612-monsoon.html). A good explanation of summer and winter monsoons and where they occur.

Pacific Island Travel, Nature Gallery: Monsoons, Tropical Storms and Tornadoes (www.pacificislandtravel.com/nature_gallery/monsoonsandstorms.html). Explains how changes in Earth's atmosphere can lead to a variety of natural phenomena, including monsoons.

PBS, Nature: Monsoon (www.pbs.org/wnet/nature/monsoon/html/intro.html). An informative site that discusses how monsoons form, where they are most common, and how people welcome them and also fear their destructive effects.

Weather Wiz Kids (www.weatherwizkids.com). Although this site is not specifically related to monsoons, it provides excellent information about climate and weather-related phenomena. Developed by New Orleans meteorologist Crystal Wicker, it is designed to help kids understand weather and why it changes.

Index

Africa, 10, 34
air, 14–15
air molecules, 15
air pressure, 14–15
animals, 25–27
Antelope Canyon, 12
Arabian Sea, 8, 17
Arizona, 10–11, 12
Asia, 4, 25, 34
Australia, 10

Bangladesh, 34
Bay of Bengal, 17
Beijing, 10
birds, 26–27
Bonn Om Touk, 25

Cambodia, 24–25
canyons, 12
carbon dioxide, 36–37
chaukas, 38
China, 9–10, 28–29
climate, 12, 13, 19–21
clouds, 16
computer modeling, 32–33,
    34
condensation, 15–16
conservation, water, 37–38
crocodile, 27
crop yields, 34

deaths, 12, 27–28, 29–30

downpours, torrential, 4–5, 33
drought, 29–30
dry monsoons, 21
dust storms, 9–10, 10–11

elephants, 26
equator, 19

famine, 29–30
farming, 27, 33–34
festival, 25
fish, 25
flash floods, 11, 12
floods, 7, 12, 16, 22, 27–28,
    28–29
florican, 26–27
forecasting, 31–34
fossil fuels, 37
freshwater, 23

glaciers, 37
global warming, 36–37
Gulf of California, 10
Gulf of Mexico, 10

haboobs, 10–11
heat, 13–14, 19
high-pressure system, 15, 21
Himalaya Mountains, 18, 19
Huaihe River, 28–29
humidity, 15
ice formations, 37

Picture Credits

About the Author

Peggy J. Parks holds a bachelor of science degree from Aquinas College in Grand Rapids, Michigan, where she graduated magna cum laude. An avid fan of all things related to earth science, astronomy, and the environment, Parks has written more than 50 books for Thomson Gale's KidHaven Press, Blackbirch Press, and Lucent Books imprints. She lives in Muskegon, Michigan, a town she says inspires her writing because of its location on the shores of Lake Michigan.